J.J. Counsilman

Noir

Blues

ISBN: 978-1-943570-22-5

Published by Gadfly Books (Glastonbury, CT, USA):
www.gadflybooks.com

Email: *publisher@gadflybooks.com*

Contents

Blues is the
who, what, when, where, and why
of sprinkling salt on a dreamer's tail.

Introduction

Noir Blues presents minimalist prose and poems drawn from blues lyrics and the wider world of bad news.

The prose describes old blues songs and a barrelhouse tragedy. The poems are presented in a variety of forms, including free verse, quatrains, *senryu, tanka,* and *choka*. The Japanese forms are well-suited to minimalism because they consist of 5 and 7 syllable lines and, except for *choka*, only three or five lines. *Choka* can be any odd number of lines beginning with seven.

The overriding similarity between blues and poetry is rhythm. Blues lyrics rhyme, as does much of poetry. Although the Japanese forms weren't created for rhyming, both the 5-7 syllable pair and the 7-7 syllable pair that ends both *tanka* and *choka* have been called primitive rhythmical units. Blues songs enhance rhythm with repetition of lines, two or three times at the beginning of stanzas, and repetition of refrains.

Blues is also dissimilar to poetry. Unlike poems, blues lyrics rarely contain odd sentence constructions, uncommon images or language, heroic deeds, fantastic events, religious symbols, and the glories of nature.[1] The lyrics are tied to external sounds, and their basic unit is the couplet with each line having a caesura and no enjambment. Thus in general blues is less sophisticated in content and presentation. It is still rich enough in emotions and behavior to allow a great variety of minimalist poems.

Here primitive blues meets primitive poetry.

Classic Noir Songs

Thirty-five blues songs from the 20s, 30s, and 40s inspired poems (which may or may not relate directly to the song). The songs are described briefly and accompanied by a QR code to an early if not the first recording.

Racism and Crime

Lyrics of racism and crime are common among old blues songs, and here are some poems with those themes.

Amended Lines

Here are poems adapted from floating lines, lines common across at least a few old songs. Many of the poems are sarcastic because the original lines were silly, trite, or exaggerated.

Still Blue

Here are poems with a wide variety of blues themes, from songs and not.

Longer Tales

Here are four tales with blue shadows: Swapping scars, a depraved legacy, the last night of a barrelhouse, and the vengeance of two abused women.

Respite From Noir Blues

Not all blues is anguish and strife.

Did your parents
say you were special?
Did they praise
your every success?
Did they suffer
your every misfortune?
Did they clean
your every distressful mess?
Nearly all less, from
heartache to murder, is an
introduction to the blues.

❧

Every living being
has family back to the
beginning of life.
How can you believe your
blues is new to the world?

Classic Noir Songs

Ed Bell

My Crime Blues (1929). A falsely accused man is convicted of murder and sentenced to death. He wants his woman to come to his trial so she can wipe away his tears after he's condemned. She doesn't need to weep and moan but needs to find someone to pay his bond. But there's no fine and he must get ready for the electric chair.

Road to Crime

Like you, I'm a dance
between limited potential
and limited chance.
And like you, I'm sometimes shamed
for acts I'm unjustly blamed.

It began with my
DNA dogging me every
step of the way
as an indelible book
that prejudiced brains to looks.

I forgot my birth,
but my subconscious knew
its veiled worth and
leaked dreams foretelling a debt
I will never forget.

I wasn't breast fed,
and can only imagine
where its absence led:

Noir Blues

Plastic and glass made me cleave
social bonds I needed to weave.

Home was the first school
of many that taught me to be
an impotent fool.
I fledged knowing untrue things
on allegedly true wings.

Teachers said to be
healthy, wealthy, and free
God and work were key.
But people lied and cheated.
In all I was defeated.

The heat of revenge
burned away the tyranny
of my DNA
and stripped the despised guise
of my inherited lies.

But freedom can't cure
what only tough love assures.
An angel languished
nearby, but I had no tools
to let in the sky.
So retribution's debris
set an earthy course for me.

Tommy Johnson

Canned Heat Blues (1928). Johnson sings canned heat (denatured and jellied alcohol) is killing him. If it doesn't, he'll never die. He uses alcorub *"to take these canned heat blues,"* meaning he sniffs rubbing alcohol to prevent delirium tremors. Later in the song, he drinks *"Jake's alcohol"* (Jamaica Ginger) because brown skinned women don't do the easy roll. He ends by asking somebody to take his canned heat blues.

Sometimes

In vino veritas
is a sty where so-called truth
is a pig that flies.

In vino veritas
is a sty where empathy
is a pig that lies.

In vino veritas
is a sty where affection
is a pig that cries.

In vino veritas
is a sty where friendship
is a pig that dies.

𝄞

Canned heat will give you
the jake-limber-leg and
brain-damage blues.

Hociel Thomas

Muddy Water Blues (1946). She's tired of trying to get along with her cheating man and would rather drink muddy water and sleep in a hollow log. She's booked for the electric chair, but he won't be there to hear the church bells ring or "*shake that thing*." Though he's already gone, she sings his stuff still suits her.

Regret

I don't regret
drinkin' muddy water
than tryin' harder.

I don't regret
sleepin' in a hollow log
'fore I'd be your dog.

I don't regret
claimin' what belongs to me
ain't never free.

*

I regret
waitin' to hear the bells ring
and the lights sing.

ɤ

God, take me instead.
Her death is beyond the blues.
My music is dead.

Robert Johnson

Me And The Devil (1937). Robert and I go for a walk during which he confesses he'll beat his woman until he's satisfied, though he blames me for her complaints about being dogged. He wants to be buried beside a highway, then doesn't care where, and finally chooses the highway so his *"old evil spirit can catch a Greyhound Bus and ride"*—presumably hell, though he doesn't say.

Satan's Blues

I want to know, how can Satan have the blues?
You're the very embodiment, of very bad news.

It gives me the blues, to lose a single soul.
Nothing should escape, the ultimate black hole.

You must understand, my contract with God.
To the hated I punish; to the loved I spare the rod.

At the beginning of hell, is purgatory's room,
where souls mourned above, escape my Doom.

Among hell's souls, is a man of twenty-seven,
a man whose blues, is his stairway to heaven.

Why did God put him, in hell's purgatory?
What was so depraved, it tarnished His glory?

The Lord kept track, of his real and sung crimes.
With one exception, they earned him little time.

It was the contract, the soul-for-mastery trade.
Only God decided, the last place souls stayed.

Noir Blues

Call me a hypocrite, I've been called worse.
His music being dear, is a blessing and a curse.

❧

He'll pursue life
until it wearies of its
own existence.

❧

God chastised me
for being overzealous
in Purgatory.
I mocked back,
I know why
you're afraid of my deeper Hell.
Every soul there has had at least one
kind thought,
decent action,
or wish of love;
which isn't much less than
your standards,
especially considering,
—forgive me for reminding you—
you alone know all causes,
which pretty much makes you responsible
for EVERYONE here.

❧

Is it possible
no soul in hell will burn
forever?

Lil Green

Knockin' Myself Out (1941). She's knocking herself out, "killing" herself, by smoking gauge. The police show up, but the Captain says, *"Kill yourself...knock yourself out, Lil, gradually by degrees."* She never used to smoke or drink, but it's the only way she can ease the pain of losing her man.

Easing The Pain

I needed a knock out
short of a checkout
while self-preservation
was still in doubt.

It had to be sweet
to make him obsolete.
So I became a voyeur
of every treat.

Cost of some stopped me
and danger I could foresee.
But one was right
for passion's debris.

The first high made me see
a needless dependency
on an needy man
who needed too much of me.

The loss of his touch
that hurt so much
was stoned by visions
of a new lover's clutch.

Noir Blues

I was primed for the news
losing love is the blues.
Ma, Bessie, and Minnie sang
all lovers paid dues.

Son House

Preachin' The Blues (Part 1) (1930). He's going to be a Baptist preacher so he doesn't have to work. He got religion that very day, but women and whiskey wouldn't let him pray. If he had his own heaven, all his women would have a long happy home. He loves his baby as much as he loves himself, but if she won't have him she won't have anyone else.

Slave and Grave

to force a choice between slave and grave?
How did her love become so depraved
the thought of which made me cry.
She meant live with her or die,
you won't have anybody."
"If you won't have me,
My woman said,
"If you won't have me,
you won't have anybody."
She meant live with her or die,
the thought of which made me cry.
How did her love become so depraved
to force a choice between slave and grave?

Edmonia Henderson

Dead Man Blues (1926). Although the song is a death threat for infidelity, the only evidence is a dream, the meanest thing she's ever seen. She dreams of her girlfriend finding her man with another woman. *"They'll set you crazy, those dang drop dead man blues."*

Drop Dead Blues
She wants to tell you
about awful and fearful blues,
the drop-dead man blues.

If you were ever blue,
mean, and hateful too, you'd know
the drop-dead man blues.

They made her curse her ma
and slap her pa in the jaw,
the drop-dead man blues.

A dream of her man
with another gal began
the drop-dead man blues.

From the start, she felt
murder in her heart singing
the drop-dead man blues.

ᕥ

Every night in dreams
promiscuous bits of my mind
become lovers.

Alice Moore

Black And Evil Blues (1929). She's black and evil but didn't make herself. She believes God put a curse on her because no-good women steal every man she gets. This time, she declares, her man will have her or no one. *"Because I'm so black and evil, yeah, might make a midnight creep,"* she's going to get a bulldog to watch her while she sleeps.

Colorism in the Blues

I was standing on the corner
talking to my brown,[2]
or
jet-black
coal black
black
dark brown
dark brownskin
dark-complexioned
darkskin
darky
brownie
brownskin
sealskin brown
coffee-colored brown
fair brown
high brown
yellow
high yellow.

Y

If the mother of
us all came from Africa,

Noir Blues

I'm black as well.

It's not my fault
my color comes from the rape
of an ancestor.

❧

I see the man called
The Son of Satan on Earth
using my measure
to carefully hang the rope
not too high and not too low.

Henry Thomas

Bob McKinney (1927). Bob threatens to put a .38 bullet in a woman's head if she doesn't hurry to him; threatens to take the life of a man who is causing trouble between Bob and his wife; and tells the High Sheriff if he had another load they would have some fun. The singer repeatedly sings, *"Wasn't he bad."* In the rest, he begs for a woman to take him back and he's *"lookin' for that bullet lay me down."*

Wasn't She Bad
Bob was a thug
with an ugly mug who was
violent when drugged.

When Bonnie arrived
at the local dive, she wasn't
taking Bob's jive.

She said no
and told him to blow
before Clyde showed.

Bob was a cur
who tried to slap her,
but she demurred.

Bonnie chose to fight
the repugnant sight with a knife,
which took a bite.

Bob lost an ear,
but Bonnie just jeered, and said
"I should kill you here."

Before she could explode,
Clyde showed and demanded
they hit the road.

Bonnie and Clyde
needed to hide. The APB
was nationwide.

Bessie Smith

Nobody Knows You When You're Down And Out (1929). She treats her friends to bootleg liquor, champagne, and wine; but when the money is gone so are her friends, and she's no used to a man. If she gets back on her feet, she'll hold on tight *"until them eagles grin"*—or not, if she meets her long-lost friends.

Lonely Cruise Blues

Without memories,
loneliness wasn't half bad.
They contained half
of all the despair I had.
To kill that half,
I fed many addictions
that produced two
lingering contradictions.
Alcohol and drugs
crafted the catch-22
of me needing
a woman wanting a man
with a sober view.
Worse than the catch-22
was the paradox
of blues easing loneliness
but keeping me on the cruise.

Maggie Jones

North Bound Blues (1925). She's going north to New York where there're no hardships like in Tennessee or Jim Crow laws like in Arkansas. In the north, she'll be free, but only her man can kill her north bound blues.

Damn Yankees

When Jim Crow came,
were you scared for your veiled
racist game?
Did you hide behind States' Rights?
Offload your bias
on the South after the fight?
Wasn't white privilege
what the war was about?
Did you abandon
blacks to let the beast back out?
What was left to believe?
Had you stayed or Lincoln lived,
we'd all be white free?

Here are more songs of racial injustice:

Cow Cow Davenport
Jim Crow Blues (1927). He's leaving a Jim Crow town for Chicago, where money grows on trees and he doesn't need his woman. If the weather doesn't suit him or he can't find a job, he'll go back to the Jim Crow town and ask for his old job back.

Leadbelly

Jim Crow Blues (1930). He finds racism everywhere he goes. He makes several pleas *"to break up this old Jim Crow,"* and identifies movies as having a lot of Jim Crow.

Josh White

Jim Crow Train (1941). White sings *"This train is Jim Crow,"* and wants to stop the train and Jim Crow so he can ride. At the end, he speaks, *"Damn that Jim Crow."*

Sippie Wallace

Jack O' Diamonds Blues (1926). Her gambling man is cruel and keeps her broke. He stole all her money, cut up all her clothes, and tired to put her outdoors. He traveled the whole world but found nothing pleased him.

Gambler's Blues

You've got Gambler's Blues
when flush with money you seek
a sweeter honey.

You've got Gambler's Blues
when your eyes are on the prize,
never on the price.

You've got Gambler's Blues
when the reward's a short high
for the lust in one eye.

You've got Gambler's Blues
when your family's shame has
only you to blame.

You've got Gambler's Blues
when drugs and booze make you
pay toxic dues.

You've got Gambler's Blues
when addiction makes you sing
to beggars or kings.

Hazel Meyers

Pipe Dream Blues (1924). The singer has happy dreams in poppy land until she's woken and gets the mean pipe dream blues. She burns ten thousand dollar bills every time she lights her pipe; and someone woke her up for their amusement.

Pipe Dream Blues

Imagine returning
from a dream picnic to
constant hunger.

Imagine returning
from a dream lover to
someone you hate.

Imagine returning
from dream prosperity to
dire poverty.

Imagine returning
from dream creativity to
dull reality.

*These are the dues
one must pay for addiction
to pipe dream blues.*

ɣ

On rare occasions,
I sense a faint enchantment
between sleep and awake

Noir Blues

and am left in despair because
it's my only magic
I will ever have.

Bukka White

Parchman Farm Blues (1940). He's been sentenced to life on Parchman Prison Farm, and sings about leaving his wife in mourning, meaning no harm to any man, and working from dawn to sunset. He continues about wanting to go home and hoping to overcome his ordeal.

Parchman Farm for Women

Blood from iron shackles;
sexual abuse by guards;
food that sickens;
ruined shoes, menstrual rags,
soiled, reeking clothes;
families that don't care;
nights of crying,
coughing, spitting, dreaming, sex;
mosquitoes, bedbugs
enflaming skin and tempers;
snakes that kill and ticks
causing oozing infections;
stinking latrines;
dumps feeding hordes of mean rats;
vicious hatreds;
dangerous stupidities;
dreams with no beauty;
failure to find or be a friend;
and deaths of those who tried to flee.

❦

Parchman Farm prison
would be a model of hell,
except it may be worse.

Big Bill Broonzy

Sun Gonna Shine In My Door Someday (1935). Through a series of woes, including being hungry, broke, friendless, a woman's dog, and in jail again, he's optimistic about the future. At the end, he gets an unidentified revenge on a buddy.

Winners and Losers

In *Good Woman Blues* (1936), Peetie Wheatstraw sings:

His woman keeps him clean,
and when he's down and out, she
doesn't treat him mean.

In *Early Morning Blues* (1926), Blind Blake sings:

It ain't no lie,
the day his woman quits him
is the day she dies.

In *My Mellow Man* (1941), Lil Green sings:

Her man doesn't steal,
but comes home every day
for his meal.

In *Tricks Ain't Walking No More* (1930), Lucille Bogan sings:

When money is tight,
you gotta rob and steal
to ease your plight.

In *Honeymoon Blues* (1937), Robert Johnson sings:

With a license in hand,
they'll honeymoon in a
long distant land.

Noir Blues

In *Saturday Blues* (1928), Ishman Bracey sings:
His woman's mean.
When he asks for water, she
gives him gasoline.

In *Take Me For A Buggy Ride* (1933), Bessie Smith sings:
When her man kisses her,
she gets a feeling that's fine
up and down her spine.

In *Head Cuttin' Blues* (1937), Kokomo Arnold sings:
Black cat's under his bed.
When he gets drunk, his woman
wants to cut his head.

ϒ

Because so little matters anymore,
my blues has become mellow
with a concomitant loss of message.

Memphis Minnie

Me And My Chauffeur Blues (1941). She wants her chauffeur to drive her downtown, and not drive other girls around or she'll steal a pistol and shoot him. She declares she must buy him a V8 Ford to drive her around the world.

Genetic Upgrade

Get Genome Kits <u>here</u>.
Want more than a tune-up?
Consider our
Personification Kits.
As a blues lover,
which your DNA shows,
you'll be delighted
to hear about the discount
on **Bluesman Special!**
You can play like Bo Carter,
Big Bill Broonzy,
Sister Rosetta Tharpe, or
even, dare I say,
Lonnie or Robert Johnson!
All quite legal.
If you wish another art,
which I don't advise,
we own codes of most artists.
First consider this:
Our analyses reveal
your DNA
is a brilliant match with
Memphis Minnie's DNA.

"One Bluesman Special!"

Big Bill Broonzy

Starvation Blues (1934). He's starving in his kitchen, has a rent sign on his door, and if his luck doesn't change he won't have a home. When he had money, his doorbell rang every day. With none, his friends go the other way and he's the only man starvation knows.

Proximate Misfortune
Hard times everywhere;
never been such times before,
with begging door-to-door.

I'm the Spanish Flu.
Some say God, some say Satan
sent me to punish you.

Whether drought or flood
swept the south, the blues sang
of death and rain.

❦

Ultimate Misfortune
Death is ever black
with as little play forward
as it does play back.

Johnny Shines

Jim String (1972). This is an intriguing tale, sung and spoken, of a pimp and one of his women. Jim warns Lulu to stay away from a particular man, and when she doesn't he shoots her. He flees with his friend Red Sam but both are caught. Red Sam gets 100 years and Jim gets 99—the reason is inaudible.

Escape
A few black men
must have escaped mobs, snitches,
trackers, bloodhounds, and
white men on horseback with guns,
whips, ropes, and torches.
Like the men who were caught,
they committed
felonies, misdemeanors,
racial insults, or nothing.

Bo Carter

Old Devil (1938). He beats his baby with a rope and a line until she goes stone blind because some lowdown scoundrel has been fishing in his pond. He has no used for a woman who can't rob and steal.

Point of View

I'm the Devil.
Nothing's sacred; everything's obscene.
I dispense injustice to men, women, and the in-between.

I'm the Devil.
Nothing's sacred; everything's obscene.
Your mea culpas are neither heard nor seen.

I'm the Devil.
Nothing's sacred; everything's obscene.
Your soul is an innocuous vaccine.

I'm the Devil.
Nothing's sacred; everything's obscene.
Even God doesn't give a damn your life's been mean,
obviously.

❦

The Devil is busy.
They ain't nothin' the Devil can't do.
[Lightnin' Hopkins *Devil Is Watching You*]

Mississippi John Hurt

Frankie (1928). It's the story of Frankie shooting Albert 3 or 4 times because, in those immortal words, *"he's my man and he done me wrong."* This rendition of the classic is unusual if not unique in the judge claiming Frankie's *"gonna be justified. Kllin' a man, and he did you wrong."* It's far more likely she'd be sentenced to death.

Taleless

Frankie is not a tale
but a question:
Under what conditions
would the betrayal of a lover
be worth two lives?

❦

*"She used to be so pretty,
now she can't remember her own name."*
[Country Joe & the Fish *Crystal Blues* (1969)][3]

Ida Cox and Lovie Austin

Graveyard Dream Blues (1923). In a dream, she goes to the graveyard and asks the gravedigger for her man back but is told he has said his last goodbye. Then she wakes to *"only a dream."*

Heroines

I won't tell you
a tale of great courage
and pure virtue
and wake the heroine.
The masses think it
a cheap trick, but wouldn't
if they understood
there's no such thing as "just a dream."
A heroine
may live in a palace
when she sleeps,
but has the same heroic soul
whether she lives
in a palace or farm house
when she wakes.

❧

Savior of Sanity

It's said without dreams
we would all be insane.
But how can that be?
If dreams can encourage madness,
if few are remembered,
if few have meaning, where is
the savior of sanity?

Noir Blues

No more you and me
is what my dreams can
foresee:
Infidelity.

I quickly learned
she was a fiend misbegotten
in my hopes and dreams.

When seeking revenge,
I never dream of two graves,
only the debt paid.

No memory fades
faster than the memory
of a dream.

My dream laughter
is better medicine than
my woken laughter.

Has a believer
ever dreamed of committing
suicide in Heaven?

If dreams are
secretions of the soul,
I'm leaking nightmares.

*"When so ever you
have a dream, always take
your
dream the other way."*[4]

Kokomo Arnold

Bad Luck Blues (1938). He's had troubles all his days, one with a woman who has ways like a wild cat in the woods. He's scared to stay and scared to leave the bad luck town; but he doesn't want anyone's advice. He's going back to the woman who treats him right. He would rather kill his sister and brother than let a woman wreck his life.

Odds

It's my bad luck
not one of your ancestors
in 4 billion years
died before breeding.
What are the odds of that?

❧

Here are 7 more songs titled *Bad Luck Blues*:

Sonny Boy Williamson – His cousin is dying from being shot.

R.L. Burnside – His woman left him, and now he only craves whiskey and women.

Albert King – His woman took his money and left, and he's lonesome.

Robert Welch – He's been driven from door to door, and he misses home.

Lightin' Slim – Police put him in jail and turned him to the wall.

Ma Rainey – She might as well die because she can't get the man she loves.

Blind Lemon Jefferson – He has lost all his money gambling.

Mississippi John Hurt

Stack O'Lee Blues (1928). The song is a linear tale from Billy de Lyon pleading for his life to Stack O'Lee being hung for murder over a $5 Stetson hat.

Stagolee[5]

I got up 'bout four.
Stagolee an' big Bully
done have a fight
'bout dat raw-hide Stetson hat.
Stagolee kill dat Bully.

Stagolee shot Bully.
Bully fell on de flo'.
Bully cry out,
"Dat fohty-fo' hurts me so."
Stagolee kill dat Bully.

Sent for de wagon.
Wagon don't come, loaded
wid pistols an'
dat big ole gatlin' gun.
Stagolee kill dat Bully.

Some giv' a nickel,
some giv' a dime, I didn't give
a red copper cent,
'cause he's no friend o' mine.
Stagolee kill dat Bully.

Carried po' Bully
to the cemetary ground.
Preacher say Amen,

and they lay po' body down.
Stagolee kill dat Bully.

Fohty dollah coffin,
and eighty dollah hack went
to cemetary
but failed to bring him back.
We all dodgin' Stagolee.

Y

Billy's Plea

Billy pleaded with Stack to spare his life
for two babies and a loving wife.
Billy should have guessed
Stack's empathy was repressed:
A man threatening death over a hat
has no more conscience than a sewer rat.

To put Stack at ease,
here are 5 other ways to appease.

1.
Bribery:
Offer hats, women, or booze
generously.

2.
Flattery:
Play up some trait
as mastery.

3.
Joke:
Say he's a fun guy,
and don't choke.

4.
History:
Speak of his reputation
with sophistry.

5.
Consequences:
Alluding to hanging
should jar his senses
(though which way,
who can say).

Helen Gross

Bloody Razor Blues (1924). With murder in her eyes, the day she sees her lowdown man is the day he dies. She's going to carve him deep down to the bone and bleed his heart until it runs dry. Her razor is bloody and her hands are running red. He trifled with her best friend.

She vowed to bleed him
if he cheated one more time
and call his blood wine.

Why and Who

The song is brutal from beginning to end and has not the least love, hope, regret, or consequences.

My questions are: Why would anyone compose it? Who would record it? Why would Helen Gross sing it? Who, by the title, would buy it?

My quess is: The composer, producer, singer, and buyers all wanted retribution against a man or woman for cheating.

Blind Willie McTell

Death Cell Blues (1933). He's accused of murder but hasn't harmed a man; of burglary but hasn't raised his hand; and of forgery but can't write his name. The judge won't give him a fine, and only the father time will release him.

Innocent

Accused of murder,
he ain't never harmed a man.
He's a saint, it seems.

Accused of forging,
he can't even write his name;
or so he claims.

❧

Guilty

They gonna fry me
as soon as the lights go out.
Then it's *"Goodnight moon."*

The thought of a rope
strangles my soul. *"Give the shysters
my silver and gold."*

Robert Johnson

32-20 Blues (1936). If his woman doesn't come or is unruly, he'll cut her in two with a 32-20,[6] with support from a Gatling Gun. He's angry over her staying out all night and seducing him while she had another man. He can't take his rest with a 32-20 against his breast.

Kill or Disarm

A Gatling Gun sounds ominous, as does sleeping with a gun bigger than his woman's .38. That's two suggestions of violence against none of consequences. Even knowing that, I would like a resolution: Does he or does he not take his rest?

ɣ

She undressed
as I rewrote my will.

Big Boy Edwards

Louise (1934). After being sentenced to work on a county road, he looks for Louise to bring his bail. His crime isn't identified, but a man on horseback counts him every hour to see if he'd run away. He sings, *"Looked in her face, and I looked down in her hands, was Louise comin', comin' to get her man."*

A Short Story

Sentenced on the road
for an unidentified crime,
I must pay a fine.

Guards on horseback
count me every hour hopin'
I'd run away.

Along comes Louise
with bail in her hand and
a wife's reprimand.

ɣ

If the blues don't kill me, boys, I'll never die.
[Frank Hutchison *Worried Blues* (1927)]

Blind Blake

Third Degree Blues (1929). After he's arrested (for an undisclosed crime), the police beat and kick him and give him the third degree. He's put in a cell without clothes or shoes, which is why he's screaming the third degree blues.

Under A Blue Moon

I stepped on his foot
and kept it pinned as I struck
under his chin.
I punched his solar plexus,
which left him breathless,
unable to whine or protest.
I released his foot,
and with left hand over right
struck palms to chest
with considerable might.
His head crashed against
a wall, leaving a trail
of blood marking his fall.
His partner telegraphed a punch,
but a jab to the throat
with a sharp kick to a shin
wiped away his grin.
He was too drunk to feel much,
so I struck again.
My fist rose above his head;
an elbow came down
and cracked ribs too well fed.
I grabbed his crotch;
a strike could make his balls explode
(or so I've been told).
The image was so ugly,

Noir Blues

I dropped him in the road.

*

Once in a blue moon,
would-be rapists are caught
by someone able
to execute an assault.
Once in a blue moon,
justice is not in despair, though
it's a shame blue moons are so rare.

Lonnie Johnson

She's Making Whoopee in Hell Tonight (1930). Johnson sings about cutting his woman's late hours with a razor and giving an undertaker her height and size. He follows with a condemnation of death that leaves much to the imagination: Making whoopee in hell with the devil. The singer whines about being her slave but declares that although the devil has 90,000 women he needs one more.

Cosmic Black Holes

Bah! You fall in one of those
and you disappear
forever.
Nothing left.
*Come to the **original** black hole,*
and something survives,
albeit a soul
immensely shriveled by
hate,
self-pity,
meanness,
arrogance,
violence,
and depravities only I in the universe applaud.

You've got no right to complain,
and look on the bright side:
God may swoop down and save even you
(though, just between us, the probability
is an atom's width from Never).

❧

Noir Blues

He loves
improbabilities
of hope.

Charley Patton

A Spoonful Of Blues (1929). He's willing to fight, hit a judge, and kill over cocaine. The song is peculiar in having many incomplete lines finished by his guitar. "It's all I want, in this creation is a...".

If Not Me

I sell escapes, though insanity and death are free inclusions because my empathy was drowned in a sea of want, weighted down by good fortune and the knowledge if not me...

ɣ

All I crave, mama,
is a spoonful of the stuff
that's never enough.

Billie Holiday

Strange Fruit (1939). A lament about the lynching of black men in the South. *"Here is a strange and bitter crop."*

Robes and Hoods
10 armed white men
in white robes and hoods meet
10 armed black men
in white robes and hoods at night
by accident
on horseback on a dirt road
in Mississippi.
Hot rain suffocates the night;
clouds darken the moon;
a Barred Owl hoots curses; and
a Whippoorwill sings of death.

*

Judge, you're gonna grant bail? He's as guilty as sin.

Sam, it's a year's pay for his family.

I'm worried about letting him loose. I've seen plenty of madmen, but *this* one. And his family.

How about this? If they get the money, we keep it *and* him. Of course, you'll have to file a separate charge. And I can set bail on that as well. Line up the charges, Mr. District Attorney.

Good joke, Judge. We'd both be dead in a week. Have they threatened your family yet? You know they will.

No, but the accusers are terrified and the Sheriff's ready to panic. Everyone believes the whole family are killers, and everyone may be right. We need a permanent solution for the lot of them. We could use a black posse about now.

They'd have to go at night and wear white robes and hoods. What do you think would happen if they met a group of white men in white robes and hoods?

Hell would descend on Mississippi and spread like a disease.

Bessie Smith

Young Woman's Blues (1926). She's a young woman who isn't done running around. Although she's a deep killer brown and not a high yellow, she's as good as any woman in town. Her goal is to drink good moonshine and "run these browns down," though the mention of a long, lonesome road suggests her life hasn't always been filled with men.

Miscegenation
of quite different creations
can create great joy
with merciless beguile in
paradoxical smiles.

Blind Lemon Jefferson

Hangman's Blues (1928). The song is a graphic account of a hanging, from sight of the gallows to gasping for breath. Although he admits he's a good-for-nothing killer, the last line has the nasty twist of him knowing a trifling woman is going to celebrate his death. It's a blues masterpiece.

Insanity or Instinct

Rejected stalkers want to reconcile
intimate relationships turned hostile.

Resentful stalkers feel humiliation
and want revenge as vindication.

Intimacy stalkers have a loneliness
that identifies non-existent love as harmonious.

Incompetent stalkers live in solitude and lust
through incompetence at building social trust.

Predaceous stalkers are sexual deviants,
men seeking the sexually expedient.

*

I suspect
all 5 are perversions
of the instinct to stalk
food and enemies.

Peetie Wheatstraw

Gangster's Blues (1940). He's going to gag and bind the man who kissed his wife; take him for a ride; tear him to pieces and put him back together; and bury him out on the lonesome prairie.

Sins of the Blues

The Ten Commandments
have 5 suited to gospels
and 5 to the blues...

Murder is wrong,
but threatened or intended
in song after song.

Cheating is the star.
The anguish of betrayal
leaves a vocal scar.

Stealing is posed
as a quick recipe
for necessity.

Lying is a sin
because of its effects
on love and sex.

Coveting is rare
because it seldom has
compelling despair.

Lonnie Johnson

When You Fall For Someone That's Not Your Own (1928). He sings you don't know trouble until your woman falls for a no-good man or you fall in love with another man's wife. It's the age old problem of infidelity (which in evolutionary terms is men trying to maximize their reproduction and women trying to upgrade theirs).

Evolution Blues

I'm living blues that began with mankind.
It's blues as old as love's decline.

I'm living blues that began with sex.
It's blues as old as deceit's effects.

I'm living blues that began with trust.
It's blues as old as a man's lust.

I'm living blues that began with cries.
It's blues as old as a woman's lies.

I'm living blues with a debt to evolution.
It's blues as old as infidelity's
massive contributions.

Racism and Crime

*"They taught you the
religion they disgraced"[7]
with their betrayal.*

A Letter

Parchman Farm has cats,
so I composed a blues song
about their love
of freedom, independence,
skill, detachment,
and claws, especially claws.
What do you think of
*The Parchman Farm Stray Cat
Blues*?
I'd play it for you
except I'm not goin' in there
and you're never comin' out.

Death Threats

Many blues songs
sing of death threats to lovers.
But none sing that

- the threat can't be
  erased,
- they demand a choice
  between slavery and
  death,
- and killers often die soon.

Songs Not Sung

Old blues singers
sang of death threats and
murder,
but not of gangs, rape,
child abuse, kidnapping,
illiteracy,
bullying, insanity,
and rarely slavery.

ϒ

On occasion, slaves
learned something shameful
about their masters.
Here must be many tales
of creative vengeance.

I get Sing Sing blues
when I hear them hammers
ringing in my dreams.

The blues is filled with
songs of would-be murderers
not taking the fifth.

Rags on my back
and shackles on my legs, Lord,
just 'cause I'm black?

Noir Blues

The slave dealer said,
"One dies, get another,"[8]
like it's a bother.

.45 in hand
with a deadly legal plan
for her backdoor man.

"Jailhouse burning down!"
I wouldn't care but my gal's
a guest of the town.

90 days and nights
in a chain gang and prison cell
are a preview of hell.

Instead of when,
the Judge said I'd never see
my woman again.

Can you believe
*"12 months ain't no great long
time"*[9]
on a chain gang?

*"You've got to beat me
to keep me"*[10] are lyrics
for masochists.

Twenty-nine days
and 100 dollars
I must do and pay.

When I whipped my gal
with a singletree, she cried,
"Don't murder me!"

If I live and work
like a dog in chains, am I
a man or a dog?

Preacher in the street
seducing women he meets.
Time to cut his conceit.

I tell no lies.
My baby's not leaving
until she dies.

*"Stab him if he stands
and shoot him if he runs"* is
intended murder.

*"The undertaker
has your height and size on
file,"*
I said with a smile.

You're two times eight, gal,
and knew too well what to do.
I got *The Noose Blues*.

On my last go-round,
penitentiary bound and
too soon underground.

Noir Blues

I asked the warden
to let me go. He said, "*In
a lifetime or so.*"

At my trial,
you weren't around. News
flash:
I'm Joliet bound.

I don't wanna choose
'tween cold north and Jim
Crow blues.
Either way, I lose.

*"Judge, tell me why
30 days for vagrancy
with no jobs around?"*

He asked, but he knew
it was Jim Crow slavery
on a white man's farm.

Amended Lines

Ease my mind and
repair my soul this time, Blues!
Stop fucking around!

The seven sisters
sang sweetly in my sleep: *"You'll*
live 12 days a week."
I believe, 'cause it's been said
they can talk to the dead.

See, see rider, see
what you done done, lovin' me
till your man done come.

I love my baby,
but my baby don't love me;
a blues tragedy.

I drink 'cause I'm dry;
I drink 'cause I'm blue; I drink,
mama, 'cause of you.

The doctor declared
drink was gonna kill me, but
he didn't say when.

"Take me back, baby,
and I'll let the 19 go,"
so blues BS goes.

Nothin' I knowed, Lord,
somethin' I'd heard, of her plan
for a backdoor man.

"Blues ain't nothin' but..."
except it's never the same.
[Worst blues line ever.]

Take me back, baby,
and try me one more time.
Even a fool can learn.

I got a pistol
as long as she's tall. My gal
comes when I call.

I've done more for you
than the good Lord ever done.
I wish I'd done none.

I'm a motherless child
who knows no right or wrong.
Where were you, father?

Ain't nobody's fault
but the code of DNA
my love mutated.

Noir Blues

I'm worried now,
but I won't be worried long.
I ain't a blues song.

On Black Mountain,
gunpowder sweetens black tea,
babies cry for booze.

Another mule's
been kickin' in my stall.
Time to break a leg.

I say to fools
fishin' in my pond, I don't do
catch-and-release.

I'd go back
to my old time used-to-be,
but it would shame me.

*"Daughter on the street
selling her sweet jellyroll"*
sounds so innocent.

I'm goin' away
to wear you off my mind.
Hope it works this time.

I can get a woman
as fast as you can get a man
if cheatin's your plan.

Two women in hand.
One will have the other's man
'cause of bragging.

I rolled and tumbled
and cried the whole night
through
a woman's fool.

*"Mr. Conductor,
let a poor boy ride the blind."*
"But the train ain't mine."

You spend my dollar
like you spend your dime. It's
time
to separate mine.

*"You gotta reap
just what you sow"* belongs to
gospels and blues.

I ate my breakfast
blues in my bread foretelling
a bad day ahead.

Nobody knows you
when you're down and out if
you're a self-made bum.

You were sugar, babe,
but you ain't sweet no more.
There's a train at 4.

When I get the blues,
I'm too mean to cry. I'm
a really tough guy.

I'm good-lookin' and
an angel's angel child
who can do no wrong.

She brings me coffee.
She brings me tea. She just
can't bring
the jailhouse key.

You made me love you,
and now your man has come.
Damned if I'll run.

Getting a woman
to find you another man
is my urgent plan.

You're three times seven,
but your sister's two times
eight
and looks like heaven.

"I'm cursed by Satan,"
she laments in a song, as
her man hums along.

Blues, booze, and trouble
will follow me to my grave
'cause I won't behave.

I know who's been here
since your daddy been gone.
He left with few clothes on.

Two things I can't stand,
hypocritical preacher
and jellybean man.

You reap what you sow.
If you're lowdown and dirty,
the world's gonna know.

The Dark Gypsy said,
"You're free would-be demon.
Go, destroy the world."

T.B., let me be.
You took my gal and now
you wanna take me.

She bit a dog and
40 doggone dogs went mad,
so she claimed.

Tricks is walking slow.
Men have no money to spare
wherever they go.

If caught cheatin',
I'll regret the day I was born
her razor forewarned.

Noir Blues

Get google-eyed with
hair tonic, shoe polish, wine,
and turpentine.

Got a hoodoo hand
stopping my woman getting
another man.

Eye on my pistol;
eye on my trunk. When
sleepin',
I ain't always drunk.

Jellyroll baker,
I'll be your slave. For your jelly
I'd rise from the grave.

Rather be a devil
than that evil woman's man.
I'd need to be.

Pulled back my cover,
blues all in my bed. Nowhere
blues ain't in my head.

Trouble in mind, I'm blue.
I'd rather die than live with
half woman/half shrew.

Blues jumped a rabbit
and sang a Howlin' Wolf song
as they ran along.

Our vow was for life,
but I caught her telling
the same vow twice.

I've been down so long
a smile/frown on her face
is a bad/good song.

I caught the blues.
Papa and mama caught it too.
It's worse than the flu.

She put that thing on me
they call a stingaree. Now
I'll never be free.

Tears won't make me stay.
The more you cry, the farther
I'm going away.

Still Blue

"Blues, how do you do?"
"I'm mighty fine but foretell
big trouble for you."

The Purest Blues

Would you want to know,
by listening only,
if the blues singer
had lived the abuse, danger,
infidelity,
addiction, guilt, injustice,
racism, or loss,
he or she sang about?
It may be unbearable.

In The Park

In the park, there were
preachers, pimps, dealers,
gamblers, thieves, grifters, ex-
cons,
whores (both men and
women),
peddlers, drifters...
All the dwellers
desperate for
money, food, sex, drugs, music,
and whatever hidden from
God.

In the park, you could

preach, peddle, drink, buy/sell
drugs,
sing/play music,
tell stories, fuck, hide, gamble,
fight, steal, rob, murder, and
die.

In the park, to survive
you needed decency and
depravity.

Y

The untold story
of loneliness is being
less than half a pair.
As well as all the laughter,
smiles, love, and sex,
she took more than half the
words,
songs, smells, touches, tastes,
more than half of something
new
every shrinking day.

I've never sung
about why I was born,
why I am here,

why I am who I am, and
why I must die.
They're meaningless questions,
fit for gospels, not the blues.

She said, *"Your truths*
aren't lies no matter how hard
your history cries.
I will sing the blues for you
but not to abuse or excuse."

I can't imagine
a world where karma has
precise justice, where
cheaters are paid in kind,
and the blues is just shadows.

You'll find what's not there
if you look hard at love.
You'll find both
the not there that's missing and
the not there that's imagined.

❦

The orphanage was
a den of vipers that would
make a snake shed blood.

Among lots of cats
are lots of one-eyed rats
in sheep's clothing.

I'm a poor woman
with no lover except blues
I'd trade for a man.

He drank so much booze,
they poured him into a grave
as his band played blues.

I'm drinking booze
to give my misfortune time
to become the blues.

I don't think this bone
comes from a one-eyed cat.
The mad dog still lives.

My woman cast a spell
like a love demon from hell.
Lord, I don't feel well.

I'm goin' south where
women suit my lovin' and
weather suits my clothes.

My voodoo woman
can make love that excuses
all her abuses.

Reefer blues ain't bad?
Best damn blues I ever had!
Makes blues sweetly sad.

Noir Blues

Down the alley
against the wall. Times too
mean to be a doll.

When I first knew blues,
I didn't know what to do
except drink more booze.

I'm a travelin' man
ridin' the blinds when I can
with guitar in hand.

Been mistreated but
don't want to die. Hell has
no hope of love.

I lost everything
except blues that sings of hope
'cause it's my lifeline.

Worried blues ain't bad.
Worst damn blues I ever had!
Kind that drives men mad.

You'd be evil too.
A woman can only stand
to be so blue.

Said my mornin' prayer,
the one full of despair
'cause she wasn't there.

I packed my suitcase
and my cat. Don't ask, baby,
we ain't comin' back.

Bury me deep,
so when I die I can't hear
your bogus weep.

Was an awful scene,
drought leaving the verdant
south
with nothing green.

I asked which train,
but was afraid to ask,
"Was she alone?"

Went to a gypsy
and a voodoo woman too.
Worry, if I was you!

Can you believe
my woman's black cat bone
can
make me moan and groan?

Drinking is fine
to keep you off my mind
except at bedtime.

About half past four,
heard bangin' on my backdoor
by a husband quite sore.

Noir Blues

Woke up this mornin',
head full of wails and screams
from a drunk's dreams.

Woke up this mornin',
blues round my bed from what
the drink demons said.

Look a-here, mama,
what you want me to do?
Act like a dog too?

At Newport News,
I found my muse. Trouble
taught me
to sing the blues.

Pussy, sweet pussy,
where you been? Caterwauling
in an alley of sin?

Woman, don't raise sand.
I ain't yours to command.
Let's work hand-in-hand.

Both men and women
have jellyrolls, stingarees,
hambones, and yas yas.

You're a monkey man,
and not good enough for me.
You're not in my plan.

If you don't know your
birth name or when you were
born,
you've got primal blues.

We all want revenge,
for something small if we're
lucky.
Vengeance is a curse.

Voice, face, body lie
from most to least and need
to verify.

Suicide is death
with an implied history
of long misery.

Memories stalk me
with evil intent and no
thought of mercy.

I was in love once.
Now I'm sleeping on the run
with one eye open.

I was in love twice.
Now I'm sleeping with a gun
and both eyes open.

Alone so long,
I have a virginal mind,
ready but scared.

Noir Blues

Every pang of guilt
is a souvenir of a life
carelessly built.

Sins of the father
may fall hard on sons before
their lives have begun.

Sins of the mother
always fall hard on daughters,
innocent or not.

Life's awfully lonesome
when there's nowhere to go
with
a damaged ego.

The sun's gonna shine
on my backdoor the next time
water turns to wine.

It's hard to blame you
when abuse is all you knew
and love never grew.

I loved a disguise
who was a pack of lies
with an empty prize.

Longer Tales

All who are born die.
Isn't that enough, Lord,
to answer my cry?

ϒ

Swapping Scars

"That wouldn't be fair.
I have many, and they sing
nothing but blues.

He cut her face,
but his pleasure didn't last:
He got two years
aggravated battery
and she became a goddess.

Only a goddess could
terrify women, scare men,
dare the arrogant,
and charm the few who saw
ugliness enhancing beauty.

She quickly learned
to recognize fears, lies, hates,
and jealousies
to find those with enough scars
to see the same paradox.

Others believed
whatever she did, good/bad,
pretty/ugly,
right/wrong, the scar paved the
way.
It defined her utterly.

More cravenly,
they meant promiscuity,
guilty addictions,
and any felony she wished.
The face became the person.

*

She checked her pistol
because one scar was enough.
What would she be tonight?
Philosopher/Nymph because
the scar labelled her a wise
slut?

They listened to her,
but when they didn't hear
what they wanted
and saw no chance of sex,
they left as if offended.

*

She sat next to Joe.
"Remember me, Detective."
It was a small joke.
"I hope you don't mind.
I thought we could swap scars."

"That wouldn't be fair.
I have many, and they sing
nothing but blues."
"Though for only one, I'm
familiar with the concept."

"My gig starts soon."
He pointed to the backdoor.
"You can join me."
She followed, wanting to know
how his scars sang many songs.

Joe lit a pipe.
They passed it back and forth.
He put it away.
He raised a hand to her face
and ran a finger down the scar.

The touch was gentle
down the pits and protrusions.
She flinched. "Detective,

are you investigating
the result of a crime or me?"

"Both, because the crime
has made you more beautiful."
"That's the paradox
so few people understand."
"It must overwhelm them."

"I suppose it makes
hidden scars seem less bad."
"I would rather see
the physical origin
of the fear every scar brings."

"When do you finish?"
Sex may decide the winner.
A mugger appeared.
To Joe, he said, "Money, drugs.
I saw, and I gotta gun."

She said, "Let me first.
I have much more of both."
She turned towards him.
"Say, woman. That don't scare
me.
Maybe I take you too."

She reached in her purse
and put her hand on the pistol.
She shot the man
in his gun hand and his thigh.
He dropped the gun and fell.

Joe picked up the gun,
cared for the boy briefly,
and called 911.
He turned to Helen, *"So this
is swapping scars,
danger that created mine
setting yours free?"*
*"It will do, and your turn will
come.
Morning is far away."*

Cowboy Blues

Sprinkle salt, cowboy,
on America's tail.
It's your legacy.

Fade, cowboy, fade
to a black and white time
in TV crime.

Star, cowboy, star
in chronic stories of gun crime
in TV time.

Bleed, cowboy, bleed
the blood of a pantomime
in TV crime.

*

Gallop, horse, gallop
all day hard with no rest
in a bulletproof vest.

Chew, cattle, chew
for the East's gluttonous need.
Beware of the stampede.

Die, buffalo, die
on prairies of slaughter
for white squatters.

Fear, girl, fear
the danger you face.
The West's a mean place.

Play, boy, play
villain and Indian games.
You're Jesse James.

Pray, mother, pray
over the chance to thrive.
Wail when babies die.

Protest, woman, protest
being a lady or whore.
You have more doors.

Drink, doctor, drink
to your life as a hack, with
self-inflicted payback.

Teach, teacher, teach
though being the hero's mate
is your highest fate.

Print, newsman, print
a high-minded rag. Beware,
a low-minded gag.

Preach, preacher, preach
your simplistic morality.
It's not reality.

Hammer, blacksmith, hammer
horseshoes and wheels before
automobiles.

Serve, bartender, serve
rotgut whiskey and stale beer.
Wipe spills and tears.

Plunk, pianist, plunk
a clunky tune[11] except
when drunks commune.

Gamble, gambler, gamble
with card as harbinger. Still
hide your derringer.

Live, bargirl, live
a life of prostitution. Pray,
a bride's absolution.

Farm, farmer, farm
away from the range. Patience
with guns forestalling change.

Search, prospector, search
with a gambler's mind. Endure
the hardships you mine.

Sling, gunslinger, sling
guns with a death knell. Dread
facing a posse's quell.

Rob, robber, rob
homes, coaches, banks, and
trains,
but fear prison chains.

Rustle, rustler, rustle
the herd of another man.
Have a hiding plan.

Thieve, horse thief, thieve,
though it's a capital crime.
Flee hanging time.

Hang, hangman, hang
villains high and dry. Smirk at
dancing in the sky.

Smoke, Indian, smoke
to escape the pogram with
dreams of no white man.

Dance, Indian, dance
for warpath success, but
die for white progress.

Be, Sheriff, be
a jack-of-all laws. Enforce
the law's just cause.

Review, Judge, review
the dead or alive profile
to have more trials.

Punch, cowboy, punch
cows and man. You carry a gun
but never a plan.

Fight, cowboy, fight
weaponless contests with no
fighting finesse.

Ride, cowboy, ride
a rough trail hardening
tail and tale.

Refuse, cowboy, refuse
to give up your gun. Broadcast,
"Cowboys don't run."

Take, hero, take
lady luck as your own.
Chase villains alone.

*

The cowboy blues sings
of narrow black and white
morality.

The cowboy blues sings
of self-armed and self-help
dependency.

The cowboy blues sings
of sanctioned violence as
our inheritance.

Cowboy Rules

Picture a cowboy
standoff between James and John.
The rules are simple:
One man must draw his gun first,
and one man must die.
The man who draws first and kills
is guilty of murder.
The man who draws second and kills
is innocent.
If James draws first and kills John,
he'll be hung.
If James draws second and kills John,
he'll be a hero.
Thus the man who draws first is
hung or (rarely) shot.
The man who draws second is
dead or (rarely) lauded.
Let's call James the good guy
and John the bad guy.
James only kills in self-defense
and must pray for luck.
If John draws second and lives,
he can still be bad,
and in a hero's disguise.
He too must pray for luck.

Neither man wants to draw first,
but it's against cowboy rules.

Barrelhouse Bolero

Mosquitoes buzz continuously,
mud hens squawk frequently,
a mammoth bullfrog croaks periodically,
and a lone Barred Owl sings once
"who cooks for you, who cooks for you'll."

The owl's song is so loud, Joe thinks the bird may be inside. From his chair, he stops playing and looks up, though he knows it's too dark to see the rafters over the stage. He's not worried who cooks for him and tells the owl his danger is greater. When his grandmother told him owls were evil, he asked if their songs were curses, but got no reply.

It's twilight, but Joe hasn't turned on the lights. He resumes playing Bo Carter's *Old Devil*.

Go back old devil, and look up on your shelf.
Go back old devil, and look up on your shelf.
Go back old devil, it ain't no joke, no lie this time…
Yeah!

He plays over the background of the first staff arriving.

A car's engine growls, tires crunch gravel,
and brakes grind and squeal.
Another car adds its
engine, tire, and brake noises.
It's silent for a few seconds.
Voices erupt in greetings as men and women exit.

Noir Blues

Their feet clomp, scratch, and grate
as they move towards and through the screen door.

An inhibiting noise begins inside.

The door repeatedly bangs against a side wall
as it's flung open after the weakened spring strains to close it.
Voices, clothes rustling, bags slapping, keys and coins jingling
continue into the kitchen.
A barmen yells to turn on the lights.

Joe puts the guitar aside, stands, and moves to a panel. The downstairs lights flare on. He looks around. It would be impossible to forget the old building down to the creaks of the floorboards; but it's something people do. Because the blues is dying, so is the barrelhouse, though it's booked for one more night.

Inside, barmen and cooks begin work,
with talking, laughing, and shouting over
the clinking and banging of crates of bottles,
tinkling of glasses,
clanking and clunking of pots and pans,
crackling of fire in the large iron stove,
clomping and shuffling of feet,
and scraping and screeching of dragged tables and chairs.

More cars arrive.

Car noises are followed by helloes, questions, and answers.
Cigarette girls, bouncers, and cashiers are heard
when the screen door bangs open and shut as they enter.
Inside the commotion becomes unbroken.

Joe goes to the kitchen where the staff have gathered. After greetings, he only reminds them to be prepared for a wild last night. He goes to his office to get the cash boxes.

As the preparations wind down, the staff sit in small groups talking, drinking, smoking, and snacking.

The cracking of peanut shells and chomping of seeds
slow conversations.
The Barred Owl is heard,
but no longer the mosquitoes, mud hens, and bullfrog.

The musicians arrive.

Car sounds build and abruptly disappear.
Four men and a woman emerge.
They talk as they unload cases
carried bumping, thumping, and rubbing to the stage.
On the stage,
the harp man slides up and down his harps,
and the two guitarists strum and adjust strings.
The piano player tests the feel and sound of every key
and makes adjustments to the familiar upright.
The woman hums snatches of songs
as she orders the sheets she doesn't need.

They have no microphones, amplifiers, or music stands to adjust. They go to the bar and visit staff or sit and drink.

Patrons begin arriving.

Cars begin filling the unpaved field
with engines roaring and dying, brakes squealing,
and tires squelching in the wet ground.
A hay wagon pulled by a bellowing, unmuffled tractor arrives
and two dozen teenagers and adults whoop and jump down.

Noir Blues

The tractor's engine is replaced by
a line of cacophony moving towards the front door
and through.

Patrons order food, drinks, cigarettes, and gauge. Groups of relatives, friends, and neighbors expand and shrink.

Plates clack, utensils clink, bottles and glasses jingle.
Tables and chairs scrape and thud as they're dragged and
dropped.
Orders are yelled over the material sounds,
occasional shout, and constant drum
of talking and laughing.

Joe signals to the musicians. The singer begins with Memphis Minnie's *Drunken Barrelhouse Blues.* She's accompanied by a lone guitar.

If you listen to me good people, I'll tell you what's it all about.
If you listen to me good people, I'll tell you what's it all about.
Well, there's good stuff to share, and it just comin' out...

Few patrons are listening, but more are coming.

Two long honks of the bus from Clarksdale
are the only sounds from outside
until the bursts of voices and feet
as the riders rush the backdoor.

Among the passengers is Athena. She's wearing a light cotton dress, red, loose, and with a low front. Her belt is a man's cut to length. Although the night is moderate and will get warmer inside, she's wearing a man's jacket with rolled sleeves. It's open at the front. Her only jewelry is the gold cross between her breasts.

As she passes,
a woman sneers with hisses.
Unmarried and married men at the bar
comment to a relative, friend, or stranger.

Athena chooses a chair in the back to avoid protectors of other people's virtue. Most are women jealous of her or afraid of losing their man. On occasion it's a man who resents her outright rejection or her refusal to give a sexual refund for drinks and effort.

The band continues with Ida Cox's *Wild Women Don't Have The Blues.*

I hear these women raving about their monkey men,
about their fightin' husbands and their no good friend...

A few women sway and hum on the dance floor
or sing snatches of the slow, well-known lyrics
to boyfriends or husbands while sitting.

Athena scans the crowd. Men smile and hold up bottles and glasses. They're young, old, poor, strong...but she's not interested. A mature, well-dressed man standing near the bar observes her. Because he's not drinking, she guesses he's the owner or manager. She looks away.

The band plays Kokomo Arnold's *Shake That Thing*:

Says down in Georgia where the dance is new.

Ain't nothing to it because it's easy to do...

The boogie woogie rhythm warms the crowd.
Dancing or not, they shout shake that thing
while clapping and tapping.

Athena knows the song and turns towards the band. A man moves near and asks how much. His face is tight and voice hard, most likely, she guesses, because of a woman or women. A sign at the entrance prohibits soliciting, though perhaps he can't read. Athena says nothing but points towards the band.

Athena is moving towards the bar when the band takes a break. While she waits, the lead guitar player pushes a bottle of beer in front of her. To her, he has a less ordinary face when singing. He leads her through the kitchen and out the back door. She breaks loose when he continues more than a few yards from the door. She clutches the front of her jacket.

Her unease is lessened by
reassuring shouts and laughs
over the drone of indistinct talk
and bottles clinking.

He leans a shoulder against the wall and faces her. His name is Jimbo Taylor. He doesn't have a blues name, and asks what she thinks of Jimbo Mojo. He'll have to carry a talisman and be bothered by desperate people.

When he guesses she pointed at him because of music, Athena replies she's a singer in private house parties across Mississippi. She doesn't say why she shouldn't have pointed.

He asks if she would like to sing with the band. She must be very good, though her physical elegance could forgive a measure of quality. For here, it would be a big measure.

She declines. Jimbo finishes the beer and throws the bottle into a field. It lands with a glop. A rich man is coming for an irresistible woman.

The harp man plays and sings Sonny Boy Williamson's *Sloppy Drunk Blues.*

> Now I would rather be sloppy drunk, than anything I know.
> You know, I'd rather be sloppy drunk, than anything I know.
> You know in another half a pint, woman you will see me go.

A few dancers outpace the beat
with body movements and shouts of sloppy drunk.

Joe asks Athena to come to his office. He talks to out-of-place people hiding, searching, and soliciting.

Athena gives her name and says she can read.

That leaves the other options. Joe doesn't want pimps, gangsters, or jealous men shooting his customers. She can stay until the Clarksdale bus if she gives up her weapons. Athena removes a Barlow pocketknife from the jacket and puts it on the desk. Joe shakes his head. It's an abysmal weapon.

Joe tells Athena Jimbo is too young for what she needs. Athena nods, though Jimbo's voice coming through the walls is whispering *shake*.

Outside the office, she stands and listens. Jimbo's playing and singing Leroy Carr's *Barrel House Woman*.

> Well this barrel house woman, what makes you so mean?

Well this barrel house woman, what makes you so mean?
Well, you the meanest old woman, baby, that I ever seen.

At the next break, Jimbo buys two beers and goes outside. Athena is waiting.

Jimbo saw Joe take Athena to his office but already guessed what Joe now knows. He hands her a bottle and asks about her pursuer.

She doesn't need his protection or money. She pointed at him because she likes his singing and because a soliciting man wouldn't take no except from another man.

Why then is she here tonight.

Athena gives no answer because it's a dreadful one. She chose the obvious place to flee from Gulfport, someplace with music near her sister's. Her ex-lover not coming means he recognized the risk from her, the law, or both. If he came, her chances of surviving were poor, but she couldn't bear living in fear all day, every day.

Jimbo convinces her it's safe to perform one song outside. She softly sings Lil Green's *Why Don't You Do Right*.

You had plenty of money in 1922,
but you let other women make a fool of you.
Why don't you do right,
like some other men do?

While she sings, Jimbo imagines accompanying her as Big Bill Broonzy does Lil Green and declares he'll go to Clarksdale with her.

She calls him Jimbo Mojo, and says no.

Athena and Jimbo return to the dance hall,
to the infinity within a room,
with its actions, sights, sounds, smells, touches, and tastes
beneath its questions, answers, observations, intentions, desires,
imaginary visits to heaven or hell....

It's two in the morning and most of the crowd are drunk, stoned, or both and ready for the wildest music, dancing, and drinking of the night. The piano player begins the third set with Bill Gaither's *Georgia Barrel House*:

> I know you from Georgia, but you're all right with me.
> I know you from Georgia, but you're all right with me.
> And if you love me, I wonder what can it be.

In the dim light and fast tempo,
dancers divest themselves of unnecessary clothing
and focus on movement
with and without sexual intent.

A man peeks in the front door. When he sees no cashier or guard, he enters and is swallowed by the crowd. He moves to the back of the room.

Athena sees a slow moving shadow on a side wall. It matches a nightmare, and she's terrified. Because she had faced him with a knife of the quickly lethal kind, she's certain he's armed with a gun. With his wealth, it will be overkill, a big gun. Although unfair to Jimbo, she moves along the opposite wall towards the stage.

Jimbo is singing and playing Big Bill Broonzy's *I Feel So Good*. It's not what the patrons want, but it's what his thoughts of sex with her choose. He pushes the rhythm.

I got a letter. It come to me by mail.
My baby says she's coming home. I hope she don't fail...

The singer's exuberance excites
the loud repetition of
I feel so good, yes, I feel so good
I feel like ballin' the jack.
They shout jack.

Between tables near the stage, Athena backs up against the wall. The tables are close together and a woman objects. Athena ignores her and moves a knife sheath hidden by her jacket from her back to her front. The choices she could have made come to mind: Carry a gun, run farther, ambush him...

Athena's former lover drank more as his wealth dwindled. She saw violence coming, and it nearly came when she prepared to leave. People die being true to themselves, and she knew she'd been lucky.

The dim lighting encourages physical flirting and indistinct exposure, with concealed violence the occasional cost.

It's the man's turn to see a moving shadow, and he walks through a range of sexual displays, some specific to a man or woman of the same or other sex and some general of the available kind. Athena moves away from the wall and stops between the dancers and tables. The drawn knife is in her right hand across her stomach. She holds the left side of the jacket over hand and knife.

The band plays Washboard Sam's *Back Door,* with the rhythm guitar on washboard.

Oh, tell me momma, who's that here awhile ago?

Oh, tell me momma, who's that here awhile ago?
Yes, when I come in, who that went out that back door…

The rapid washboard clinking and clacking
drives dancers to clap and stomp,
and those sitting or standing to bang and slap
bottles, glasses, utensils…
and hands against
chairs, tables, and walls.
Variety and volume of sounds rise sharply.

He stands in front of her. She doesn't strike, though it greatly increases the risk to herself and to Jimbo if he interferes. Although she can barely see his hands, she wishes she had stayed in the darker back.

Dancers bump into him, but he doesn't care.

He moves within inches of her face and screams he should kill her, though his tone doesn't have the implied option. She smells the same breath and sees the same arrogance she had smelled and seen the last time they met. He could have crippled or killed her, she yells in his ear. Neither of them was hurt, why can't he leave it like that.

Leaving is impossible for reasons he can't explain and perhaps doesn't know. He unbuttons the front of his suit. When he puts his hand on a large gun in a side holster and awkwardly begins to withdraw it, Athena stabs him. The long, thick blade goes to the backbone. She pulls it out with a spurt of blood.

The man drops the revolver.
As he bends over with both hands holding his stomach,
blood blossoms over his shirt and trousers.

He wails in pain and disbelief.

A woman's screams are barely heard,
but when the man drops to the floor,
dancers yell in fear and soon in panic.
They scream to relatives and friends to run.

The band makes a ragged stop,
with the streams of sound ending
abruptly or hesitantly but all discordantly.
The singer's song turns to gasps.

The explosion of sound draws Joe out of the office after he quickly dons his shoulder holster and pistol. The sound means panic and panic means violence. As he locks the office, he's slammed against the door by the crowd entering the kitchen. Joe pushes his way to the dance floor.

Streams of patrons cry for mercy
as they stomp and shove towards the front and back doors.
With chairs, men smash windows nailed shut.
Tables and chairs are overturned
with their contents clattering or breaking on the floor.
Indistinct but adding to the noise are sharp creaks by floorboards.
The musicians pack quickly
and run across the dance floor to the nearer front door.

Jimbo is standing with Athena; neither is caring for the man.

Joe yells for the barman to bring towels. Joe puts them over the man's hands and gently presses down to slow the bleeding. The man is fading in and out of consciousness. More from the size of the knife than the amount of blood, Joe believes the wound is fatal. The man gives a shriek as a spinal nerve protests. While pressing and over the groans, Joe tells the barman to close the bar and kitchen. The staff can go after he collects the cash boxes. They'll be paid after the final shutdown tomorrow.

> *Staff hurriedly store bottles, glasses, and utensils,*
> *but don't bother cleaning the bar and kitchen.*
> *They hear the man's groans and noisy breaths*
> *and leave the hall's messes.*

Although Jimbo is holding the knife, the blood on Athena's hands and jacket identify her as the attacker. The gun on the floor tells Joe it's self-defense, though against that is the knife decoy.

Jimbo takes over holding the wound while Joe goes with Athena to his office. She gave the knife to Jimbo to get something dangerous out of her hand. She isn't running.

Inside the office, Joe calls the owner of the barrelhouse. He explains the situation. Joe protests the best they can do is spot check and the bouncers are always busy with drunks.

He repeats the stabbed man is dying and will die before he can get a doctor from Clarksdale. The woman is no trouble and will disappear. No one saw the attack and it was clearly self-defense.

The owner will send the Sheriff now and an undertaker in the morning. He tells Joe to clean up and in a few days they'll discuss new business, provided the night's killing doesn't have business repercussions. Joe doesn't comment. What else does he know except music and barrelhouses?

He turns to Athena and tells her to get out of Mississippi, with Jimbo if he wants.

Joe meets the staff in the kitchen and sends them off. Even without the dying/dead man, he will staying for hours.

> *Joe wearing a gun adds to their fear.*
> *They hustle out the back door,*
> *afraid to talk in the rush to their cars.*
> *Talking, screaming, and gesturing erupt*

when they're inside and driving away.

For a few minutes, the building is quiet
except for the argument with death.

In the dance hall, the man is unconscious and sputters and gargles with each labored breath. When Joe hears a car, he goes outside and sends the watchman away. When he returns, the man is dead. The dead man, stupid man should have known Athena had a dangerous will to live.

And the dead man, stupid man ruined Joe's farewell. He had wanted to play with the band; and after that, until he was alone in the barrelhouse, and long after that. What he has now is a dead, stupid man who will choose the songs.

He locks his pistol in the office, turns out all but the kitchen lights, and goes to the stage. His guitar is there. He sits and listens before playing. The sounds are natural and for the moment better than music.

Inside are creaks of wood and chirps of crickets,
and outside are gusts of wind against the building,
rustling leaves, peeping tree frogs
and the Whippoorwill's call:
whip..poorrr well,
whip..poorrr well,
whip..poorrr well.

Y

Here are more barrelhouse songs:

Mary Johnson

Barrel House Flat Blues (1929). She has barrelhouse flats in Detroit, St. Louis, and Chicago. The police find her beer and whiskey wherever she hides them. Her barrelhouse in Chicago is 15 stories high. She gives a invitation to women who want a good time.

Ma Rainey

Barrel House Blues (1923). She's got the barrelhousing blues from feeling awkfully dry. She can't drink moonshine because she's afraid she'll die. Papa likes sherry, bourbon, and outside women. Mama likes corn liquor, gin, and outside men.

Kid Bailey

Rowdy Blues (1929). He's not going to marry or settle down until the barrelhouse is torn down. When his woman weeps and cries, he tells her she has a home as long as he has one. He declares his love but sends her a letter about parting.

Rosa Henderson

Barrel House Blues (1924). Her man leaves her with the barrel house blues. She rolled a barrel last night and the night before, when her daddy comes home she'll roll the barrel no more.[12]

Y

Why can't life be long
and death be short, you so-called
benevolent God?

Elaena and Katherine

Her mind cried,
"That promise was a mistake."
Her heart tried,
"I will never break." Her body
sighed, "That's all I can take."

When Marcus invited
four gangsters to his aunt's
home,
she was angry.
Elaena whispered to him,
"After they leave, pack your
suitcase."

When the men played cards,
Marcus soon began to lose.
Elaena guessed
the result, and warned him,
"I won't be your broker."

Marcus kept losing
and believing his aunt would
pay.
Elaena doubted
the men, who were pimps and
thugs,
would take his IOU.

When they stopped,
Elaena refused to pay.
She was furious
when Tremon said, *"Be my*

whore,
and I'll forget the money."

In her neighborhood,
everyone knew the gangster's
game
of forcing relatives
to accept a relative's debt.
She refused to pay or whore.

Tremon struck Marcus
to force her to do either.
She stood fast,
though she faced violence as
well
when she tried calling 911.

Trapped, she proposed
a dangerous new game.
She bet her body
against the debt she denied
she was obliged to redeem.

The men agreed,
not expecting her to win.
But she was frantic

to keep body and soul free
from Tremon's profane
demand.

She won back the debt,
stood, and told them all to
leave.
When Tremon ordered
the men except Jamal to go,
she knew her cleverness failed.

When she ran for a knife,
Tremon threatened her,
Marcus,
and whole family.
It was a venomous threat, but
her revulsion wouldn't subside.

When she still refused,
he said, *"It's not your choice.
I like to fuck,
beautiful Elaena.
You'll keep Jamal and me
amused."*

Jamal was careless
and regretted moving close.
A slash to his arm
was proof Elaena's resistance
would be severe.

Tremon took the knife
and said, *"Bitches always pay."*
He slapped her hard

because he saw women
as pleasure and money.

Tremon expected
her to crack without the knife.
Rather she attacked.
She broke his nose and
scratched his face,
while promising to do more.

He countered with
hard punches and hard kicks
that beat her down.
She had never felt pain
so great she couldn't say,
"Stop!"

*

Her mind cried,
"That promise was a mistake."
Her heart tried,
"I will never break." Her body
sighed, *"That's all I can take."*

*

Although unconscious,
Tremon and Jamal raped her.
For the broken nose,
Tremon beat her again
and kicked her in the head.

When she woke,
she couldn't speak or stand.
She needed help
but was too damaged and

broken
to make more than a shriek.

Elaena's neighbor
heard the cry and called 911.
The two detectives,
Katherine and Joe, were
shocked
by the naked, bloodied woman.

Not breathing,
Elaena looked dead until
she gave a loud gasp.
Katherine was shaken by
what seemed an escape from
death.

EMTs arrived.
With multiple contusions,
severe concussion,
and trauma from the rape,
she won't live they said.

Elaena did live,
though doctors doubted she'd
thrive.
Katherine admired
her will because she too
had once needed to dig deep.

*

It was months before
detectives could interview her.
She was covered

with bandages and casts.
Katherine took her hand.

Elaena spoke
about saving her nephew
but not the crime.
They knew he lived with her,
but had yet to come back.

For her safety,
Katherine assured her
she would be guarded,
though would still be in danger.
Elaena said, *"I'm not scared."*

Elaena's refusal
to name her attackers
made Joe mad, as did
Katherine's refusal
to shame Elaena for that.

Marcus was found
hiding at a friend's home.
When questioned about
the assault, he claimed
innocence
and began cursing wildly.

He realized
what his aunt being alive
foreshadowed for him.
Tremon and Jamal wouldn't
trust him to be their alibis.

Marcus tried to flee.
When he grabbed Katherine's
gun,
she shot him dead.
Although her first killing, she
felt no regret for it.

Her body camera
proved protests were absurd.
But proof couldn't break
the racial distrust
racist cops had created.

To save Katherine,
Elaena named the villains.
To the media,
she described how she'd been
abused.
Tremon and Jamal hid.

Katherine invited
Elaena to live with her.
Without news for weeks,
they nurtured a loving
trust and dependency.

Although Katherine's
rapist had been killed by Joe,
she felt safe only
when wearing a gun and when
feeling ready to use it.

Joe knew Katherine
was healing Elaena and

herself through love,
but reminded Katherine
her attacker died legally.

When weeks later,
Elaena told Katherine
the men had been caught,
Katherine again felt
the draw of retribution.

She couldn't ask
Elaena not to go because
Elaena would be
responsible for every
new crime the men committed.

She wouldn't ask
Elaena not to go because
she wanted to.
Neither woman fooled herself
it was only for the good.

To the captors,
Elaena explained Katherine
was her lover.
With her, she was not police
and wouldn't make a report.

*

At the dock site
were three armed and masked
men
and two tied and gagged.
One of the armed men said,

Noir Blues

"Gun and bodies will be
drowned."

To Tremon and Jamal,
she described her injuries
and how she survived.
Through the gags, the men
screamed
sounds of the terrified.

When Katherine asked
to be first and to shoot Jamal,
Elaena knew it was
both a selfish and loving act.
She and the armed men
agreed.

Neither woman cared
for the illegality
or immorality,
only the exalted catharses
of retribution and love.

Respite From Noir Blues

Young boy/young girl
black side/white side met and made
love between the lie.

❦

Ida Cox
Wild Women Don't Have The Blues (1924)

She hears women
ravin' about monkey men
and no good friends.
They moan and groan all day 'cause
women on the square
have men cheatin' everywhere.
But wild women don't worry.

She treats no man right,
keeps him workin' day and night.
When he's kickin',
she gets full of good liquor and
walks the streets 'til light,
comes home, and puts up a fight.
Wild women don't have the blues.

She got nothin'
by being an angel child.
You better change now

and get real wild, 'cause only
wild women get by.
Wild women don't worry.
Wild women don't have the blues.

❦

Frankie Jaxon
She Can Love So Good (1938)

I see a girl so splendidly sweet.
I vow to die if we can't meet
'cause she looks so good, so deliciously good.
Everybody must want her, 'cause she looks so good.

As you enter the barrelhouse, we become quiet.
When you begin to dance, we begin to riot
'cause you look so good, so incitingly good.
Everybody wants you, 'cause you look so good.

To dance with you, a hundred boys get in line.
I wish on the blues scale, to make you mine
'cause you look so good, so pentatonically good.
Everybody wants you, 'cause you look so good.

Now you're mine, we're visiting the President.
She says, *"Young lady, you'll make the nation content*
because you look so good, so auspiciously good.
Everybody wants you, because you look so good."

We're coming home in a tickertape parade

with people yelling, *"Lordy, she's heaven made,"*
'cause you look so good, angel, so divinely good.
Everybody wants you, 'cause you look so good.

We're all alone, with time to make our vows
to be happy beyond, what the world seldom allows,
not 'cause you look so good, so transcendentally good,
but 'cause you love so fine, so cosmically fine.

ɣ

"…and I will chase the boy in you away."[13]

ɣ

Welcomed Blues
I have
no
skill,
time,
money,
bravery,
authority,
imagination,
or other weapon
to seek vengeance
for more than the fewest
lies,
insults,
betrayals,
accusations,
humiliations,
and other wrongs.

*

It's everyone's fate to be

highly (though not completely) protected
from the burden and danger of vengeance
by
impotence.

❧

I thank God
my mirror is blind
to the pain in my heart.
When I look, I still see hope.

❧

An Old Man's Blues

Characters:
Joe, Red, Unnamed woman

Place and Time:
Mississippi, *circa* 1930

*Two men are jamming blues
on a bench outside a bus station.*

RED: Joe, put down your harp and tell me about the woman.
She took your money, I bet.

Joe puts down the harmonica.

JOE: The laughs on you, Red.
She took what I let her take when I guessed she would go.

RED: You never told me how you got with her.

Noir Blues

JOE: I was sittin' here
—you were playin' down Jackson way—
and she got off the mornin' bus.
What a sight:
a fine-lookin', scared-lookin' woman.
Straight away hit on kind-lookin' me.

RED: She was turnin' tricks at the station?
Sheriff Blake
would run her ass to a cell
and take his time bringin' her before Judge Hendley.

JOE: I was curious why she was so scared.
She said her man told her to get out of Tupelo,
or he'd beat her.
She only had enough money to come here
and wanted to go to her family in Memphis.
She hadn't tricked before.

RED: She says.

JOE: It ain't much of a sellin' point, Red.
I told her Sheriff Blake would make her do tricks in a cell for free.

RED: He'd sell her yas yas to fat old crackers
because she's a high yellow.
Ha! Our Sheriff runs the safest whorehouse in Mississippi.
I wonder if those high-livin' boys get a thrill
out of fornicatin' in a jail cell?

JOE: Why else?
They could take her anywhere for a few hours.
She said she'd do whatever I wanted for two dollars.
Two was enough to get her to Memphis.

Noir Blues

RED: I hope you told her
the pimps in Memphis were the face-cuttin' kind.

JOE: I was savin' that.
I told her she had to get out of that black dress.

RED: I bet you did.

JOE: Yeah, I did,
and my wife left a few things.

RED: Because of a *real* sudden departure, as I recall.

JOE: Not another word.
She put on one of Ellie's dresses and was likely to bust out.
"Without a black dress,
I'll have to go up to each man."
Not in that, I *could* have said.

RED: So she didn't put the squeeze on you,
and you invited her to stay.

JOE: I invited her to lunch.
When I was more sure of her,
I told her she could stay until she found a job
if she cooked and didn't steal or whore.

RED: You didn't talk about sex?

JOE: After my offer, she asked why.
Did I want sex until I was tired of her and then throw her out?
All I'd lose was food.

RED: She was desperate but not stupid.

JOE: I told her this town had plenty of ladies who liked a backdoor man.
I would give her money for her cookin' and cleanin' until she got a job.
If she wanted sex,
that was up to her.

RED: Enough history, Joe. Let's play.

Both men resume playing and then stop.

JOE: Red, I'll be damned.
That's her just off the bus from Memphis.
She's not wearin' black or Ellie's dress.

A middle-aged woman with a contrite expression walks up to the men.

WOMAN: Joe, I'm awful sorry about takin' your money.
I came to give it back.

JOE: Well, that's fine,
but how have you been livin' these past few weeks?
If it's been trickin',
you know I can't take you back.

WOMAN: Joe, this is the truth.
I took the bus back to Tupelo.
I went home when Jack wasn't there
and took the money I knew he hid.
He *owed* me that.
I went to my family in Memphis.

Noir Blues

JOE: Woman, you know he's comin' after you.

WOMAN: I don't think so. He's a loudmouth drunk
and will blame one of his friends.

Joe laughs.

JOE: You're hopin' he goes to jail over the missin' money.

WOMAN: And forgets me.

JOE: I *do* miss your cookin' and…
But don't you ever steal from me again.

The woman flinches, as if slapped.

WOMAN: Or you'll tell Jack where I am?

JOE: *Praise Jesus, woman!*
I need to introduce you to a better class of people.
Let me start with my friend Red.

WOMAN: Nice to meet you, Red.
Joe, I promise. Let's go home.

Joe rises.
He winks at his friend as much to say
God is good to old men sometimes.

❧

[1] Michael Taft. *The Blues Lyric Formula.* Routledge, Taylor & Francis Group. 2006. References to nature in the blues are what you would expect: droughts, floods, and boll weevils.

[2] Henry Thomas. *Don't Ease Me In* (1928).

[3] This is the sole song not from the 20s, 30s, or 40s, but its lyrics are as anguished as those of any blues from any decade.

[4] Scrapper Blackwell *My Dream Blues* (1932).

[5] Adapted from Howard W. Odum's *Folk-Song and Folk-Poetry as Found in the Secular Songs of the Southern Negroes.* The Journal of American Folklore, Vol. 24, No. 93 (Jul. - Sep., 1911), *pp.* 255-294. Courtesy of JSTOR.

[6] A "32-20" was a cartridge of 0.32 inches in diameter and 20 grains of black powder. It could be used in rifles or revolvers.

[7] Sterling Brown *Strong Men* in *The Collected Poems of Sterling A. Brown.* TriQuarterly Books, 1980.

[8] Matthew J. Mancini. *One Dies, Get Another: Convict Leasing in the American South 1866-1928.* University of South Carolina Press, 1996.

[9] Curley Weaver *Iron Leg Blues* (1934).

[10] Trixie Smith *You've Got To Beat Me To Keep Me* (1925).

[11] Unless it's Hoagy Carmichael.

[12] Rolling a barrel is possibly a metaphor for heavy drinking.

[13] Bobby Goldsboro. *Summer (The First Time)* (1973).

www.ingramcontent.com/pod-product-compliance
Lightning Source LLC
Chambersburg PA
CBHW071816020426
42331CB00007B/1501